For Philip

1

One old
Oxford ox
opening oysters

One Old OXFORD OX

Nicola Bayley

Jonathan Cape
Thirty Bedford Square London

Also illustrated by Nicola Bayley

A Book of Nursery Rhymes
The Tyger Voyage
Puss-in-Boots

One Old Oxford Ox is a
traditional nursery rhyme
This edition first published 1977

Illustrations © 1977 by Nicola Bayley

Jonathan Cape Ltd
30 Bedford Square, London WC1

British Library Cataloguing in Publication Data

Bayley, Nicola
One old Oxford ox.
I. Title
398.8 PZ8.3
ISBN 0-224-01353-X

Printed in Italy by A. Mondadori Editore, Verona

2

Two toads totally tired trying to trot to Tisbury

3

Three thick
thumping tigers
taking toast
for tea

4

Four finicky fishermen fishing for finny fish

5

Five
frippery Frenchmen
foolishly fishing
for frogs

6

Six
sportsmen
shooting snipe

7

Seven
Severn salmon
swallowing shrimps

8

Eight eminent Englishmen eagerly examining Europe

9

Nine nimble
noblemen nibbling
nectarines

10

Ten tinkering
tinkers tinkering
ten tin tinder
boxes

11

Eleven
elephants
elegantly equipped

12

Twelve
typographical
topographers
typically
translating types

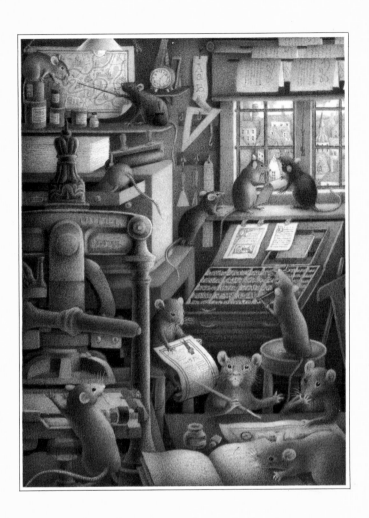